I

Dedicate this book

To

All women who would aspire to become Best Version of Themselves

# THE ART OF PERSONAL GROOMING

## HOW TO LOOK WELL GROOMED AND POLISHED

BRAMARA SHIVANNA

ISBN 979-888629132-2

# Contents

# PREFACE

Dear readers, I wrote this book to share with you all the simple, minute details of grooming that make a large impact on you and others.

The book is based on the three pillars of personal grooming. It covers every aspect of personal hygiene and grooming habits in a simple way and also explains the causes of bad grooming and its prevention. The importance of grooming in creating a good impression is explained with suitable examples.

Few chapters are dedicated exclusively to the basics of dressing, makeup, and accessories. You can learn secrets of levels of dressing for both Indian and western corporate attire along with the perceived message for each level of dressing. The book covers corporate dressing and makeup tips and their benefits. All the myths associated with grooming and a step-by-step workable plan for grooming routine is included.

This book effectively shows you how to put your best foot forward and look Well-Groomed and polished for every occasion by coordinating your outfits with matching accessories along with a suitable hairstyle and good grooming. This book is for every woman who aspires to look competent and confident and would like to elevate their look, specifically for women professionals or women attending job interviews or a trainer or entrepreneur or a mother or whoever wishes to look well-groomed and standout.

# Acknowledgements

My deep-felt gratitude to my parents, siblings, husband, and my lovely daughters for the comfort and support they provided.

My pranams to all my teachers, trainers, mentors, and Gurus who always came in timely manner to show the best path and provided me clarity on profession, passion, reality of life and shaped me up. My gratitude to Zubin Genius Trainers for helping me publish this book.

My gratitude to my friends, my batchmates, my students and my colleagues at organisations where I worked earlier. Last but not the least, my gratitude to the invisible power of almighty and universe.

# I

# INTRODUCTION TO PERSONAL GROOMING

> ***"A Good Grooming is integral and impeccable style is a must. If you don't look the part, no one will want to give you time or money"***
> ***- Daymond John***

A person is considered as well-groomed when her Personal grooming, Personal hygiene and Dressing and makeup are up to the mark. To be able to fit in society, you must make sure your personal grooming is up to the standard. In today's society appearance is more pervasive at every level of society. There are three main reasons. Firstly, most of us change home, change jobs, travel across the world more frequently than our parents and because of this, we have to re-establish our identities with new people and new environment. Secondly, the influence of social media, and television has made us judgemental about our appearance. Thirdly, the changing role of women, from homemakers to corporate women, to more challenging leadership roles. Personal Grooming is one of those things that there is no excuse not to take time and effort with as Job opportunities, relationship possibilities, and invitations to parties and other social & formal events are all linked to how you present yourself to the world.

**Grooming**

Grooming is an ***ART OF SELF PRESENTATION***. It is the process of making yourself and your appearance look neat, pleasant & attractive. Grooming also means dressing well, to be presentable to others. It simply means dressing in a way that projects an image of the sophisticated, successful working individual you are or would like to become. Grooming is a consistent act of self-care, and it should be done often to get optimum results.

**Grooming consists of 2 Aspects**

**Physical Aspect** – is all about overall Appearance, Haircare, Skincare, Makeup and Personal Hygiene.

**Metaphysical Aspect** – Is all about Personality, Body language, Etiquette, and manners

In this book, we are discussing only about the physical aspects of Grooming.

## *Personal Grooming*

Personal grooming is the act of taking care of your body through proper cleanliness and self-care. Personal grooming not only affects the way others see you but also affects how you feel about yourself. When you look and feel your best, you can present yourself confidently to others

Personal grooming means to improve one's outer and inner self to bring about a positive change to life. Everyone has a different personality that can be developed, polished, and refined.

Personal grooming and the way we look impact our lifestyle in a big way. Knowingly or unknowingly, you make a statement by the dresses that you wear and the way you are groomed and people who observe you knowingly or unknowingly read those messages.

An important aspect of Personal grooming is Personal Hygiene.

Personal hygiene involves those practices performed by an individual to care for one's bodily health and wellbeing, through cleanliness.

## *Importance of Personal Grooming*

- Personal grooming plays a vital role in reinforcing self-esteem as well as Self-confidence and improving your chances of success in many areas of your life.
- Personal grooming and hygiene help us look and feel good. It improves our physical and mental wellbeing.
- Personal grooming is essential for everyone irrespective of the gender and nature of the profession.
- The importance of personal grooming goes beyond simply looking and smelling good. Grooming is very important for us because it shows that we are focused, determined, and results-oriented.
- Good grooming is an indication to an interviewer that you pay attention to detail, and that you take care of yourself. If you don't take the time to look after your own basic hygiene or dress appropriately, that sends a

signal that you will not make an effort as an employee.

- Personal Grooming helps to understand the importance of taking care of oneself, and by doing so they become productive, because they feel vibrant and always rejuvenated.
- Good grooming is especially important if you are applying for a customer-facing position such as sales and marketing or front office executive or HR professional. The first impression you make on the interviewer is the one you will be making on the company's clients.
- Personal Grooming adds style and grace to the way one looks. Good personal presentation is something that you all can achieve and know that you look your best will give your self-confidence a big boost
- Personal grooming includes Personal hygiene and Appearance. Personal hygiene, if neglected can ruin your personality. Would you like to speak with someone who has bad breath or someone who has bad body odour or someone who has sweat stains all over his shirt or would you like to shake hands with someone with sweaty hands? I can say for sure the answer would be NO. The same goes for others as well. Even if you wear an expensive outfit, if you lack personal care, it will always let you down. Always flaunt your clean, simple yet elegant look.
- A Well-groomed person is always remembered even after meeting him or her only once. (Opposite is also true in a wrong way).

### *What doesn't mean good grooming?*

Good grooming **doesn't mean**--

- You have to spend hours in front of the mirror,
- You have to wear expensive branded clothes,
- You have to follow every new fashion trend,
- You must spend a fortune at a salon for makeup and hairdressing
- You have to buy each and every new skincare and beauty product available in the market.

# II

# THE TRUTH ABOUT FIRST IMPRESSIONS

> **"*"First impressions are important. While a book should not be judged by its cover, many people are unlikely to read it if the cover is not inviting."*
> *- Unknown*"**

In the previous chapter, we learnt about the importance of personal grooming and its benefits. Here we are learning one of the most important reasons why personal grooming is most important in ***visual communication*** by understanding the visual impressions it creates on others and how it impacts our life.

Let's take an example, consider two dishes are served to you in a restaurant, Both the dishes are prepared with same ingredients, one dish served in a bowl was decorated neatly, it looks fresh and colourful and gives out a nice aroma. On the contrary, the other dish is served in a bowl without any decoration and served as is. If we are asked to choose one, we most likely choose the one appealing to our senses, which looks good and smells good even though both the dishes are tastier. Before eating we decide which one to choose only by looking at how it was presented. We eat visually before tasting the food, if it appeals first to our eyes then only, we eat. Do you agree or not? Every day we make numerous decisions only based on external Appearance.

Let's consider one more example, imagine you are an interviewer at a company and say a young woman walks in for the interview. Her clothing choices are decent. She is wearing a white shirt/blouse and black trousers with a matching belt and shoes. However, you observe that

- Her shirt is not ironed, you can see wrinkles
- You notice a stain on her shirt
- There is a strong odour coming from her shoes (maybe his socks are not washed)
- Her hair is scattered, covering half of her face
- And lastly, when she says "Hello!", you get a bad breath

***What is the first impression of this young woman?***

Even if you carry out the entire interview diligently, you might not be able to cope with the first impression she made. It will influence your future behaviour. You might have started making snap judgements as soon as she enters the room and these judgements might have influenced your interactions with her which might not be positive.

In an interview, the first few seconds can make or break your interview. Interviewer notices poor grooming immediately, it may be difficult to recover from that first impression, no matter how good you answer. Poor grooming is just distracting.

This simple example makes us understand that we as humans have a very impressionable mind and have a high visual inclination as we have a photographic memory. We look at something or someone and within a few seconds create an impression about them in our mind and make snap judgements.

## *First Impressions - Perception people form*

As we observed from previous examples, some of the perceptions people can form solely from your appearance in a few (within 5-10seconds) seconds are--

- Your professionalism
- Your level of sophistication
- Your intelligence
- Your credibility
- Your candidature for job or promotion
- Your Financial success
- Your trustworthiness

An impression is formed in the minds of people about you, they start judging you by your looks. In 1970s Professor ***ALBERT MEHRABIAN's*** research Silent Messages proved that visual images matter a lot. He found that the impact we make on each other depends –

**55%** on how we look, Visual communication, body language, facial expressions

**38%** on how we speak, Vocal communication, tone, and pitch

**7%** on what we say, Verbal communication, the words we use

Dr.Albert Mehrabian's 55-38-7% Rule

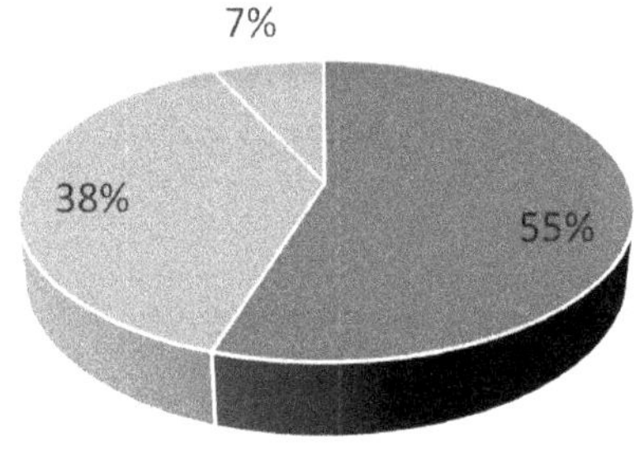


■ Body language 55% ■ Vocal-Tone 38%

■ Verbal-words 7%

55-38-7% Rule

Whether we like it or not, that is the way it is. Communicating is not a choice. The moment others see you; you start communicating. If you expect anyone to believe you are successful, creative, approachable or whatever, your image must say this before you open your mouth with your desired Visual Communication which includes your Appearance consisting of clothing, grooming, body language and etiquette.

**First Impression matters...**

- When you want to ace an Interview
- When you are meeting new people

- When you are conducting presentations
- When you are addressing large gatherings
- When you are looking for relationships
- When you are attending sales meetings with prospects

***"“You never get a second chance to make a great first impression “***
***– Will Rogers"***

Jazmin

## *Power of Personal Appearance*

As an individual living and working in highly complex and competitive society, you must recognize and understand the impact of your appearance as it communicates first to you and then to others. While it is important to like what you wear and the way you look, it is more important to understand why or why not and specifically how this affects you, others, and your life and the achievement of your goals. Universal effects of clothing and grooming are...

Your clothing and grooming affect the **way you think**

Your clothing and grooming affect the **way you feel**

Your clothing and grooming affect the **way you act or behave**

Your clothing and grooming affect the **way others react or respond to you**

We all form first impressions of the people we meet, and they can be lasting, and it takes lot of effort to change the first impressions. Many of the cues that go into a first impression are nonverbal. Dressing and Grooming are key among them along with body language and manners.

**The First Impressions** are

- Created in the first 510 seconds of a meeting or conversation.
- It gives the impression that you are competent, knowledgeable, and professional.
- A Positive First impression appeals to the senses.
- Remember first impressions are the best impressions and last long.

A well-groomed person is always prepared and ensures that any impression created of him is a positive one which is beneficial in achieving what she wants. She/he is always remembered even after meeting him or her only once (the opposite is also true in the wrong way). These are the reasons why personal grooming is the first thing to work upon when you want to create an impression.

Now you understood that first impression matters, then How to create a great First impression?

As you know first impressions are created as soon as other person notices you, what all they can see within a few seconds is your clothing, grooming, hygiene, makeup, body language and facial expressions. You are going to learn in detail everything about grooming habits, and basics of hygiene and briefly about dressing for work including clothing, makeup, and accessories. You will be learning the right way of creating good impressions to look confident, credible, and authentic.

"***"First impressions are lasting; Give special thought to your dress, your grooming, and your accessories." -Brian Tracy***"

# III

# PERSONAL GROOMING HABITS

> ***"Grooming is the secret of elegance. The best clothes, the most wonderful jewels, the most glamorous beauty don't count without good grooming***
> ***-- Christian Dior"***

The whole process of personal grooming takes place over a period of time, and it is a consistent act of self-care. Implementing personal grooming and hygiene to your routine brings a positive change in oneself and it takes a considerable amount of time to get optimum results. In the previous chapter, we understood the importance of first impressions and what are factors contribute to great impressions. Here we learn about the basic habits to take care of good grooming.

## *Pillars of Personal Grooming*

Personal Grooming involves all the aspects of your body: Overall cleanliness along with attention to makeup, hair and dressing is vital. If you work on your **visual resume** (your appearance) with all 3 pillars of personal grooming, you will become a well-groomed person. This book's focus is mainly on **1st pillar** of grooming and the remaining pillars will be explained in detail in upcoming books of the ***smart woman series***.

**Three pillars of Personal grooming** -

- Personal Hygiene and Grooming habits
- Makeup and Skincare
- Clothing and Accessories

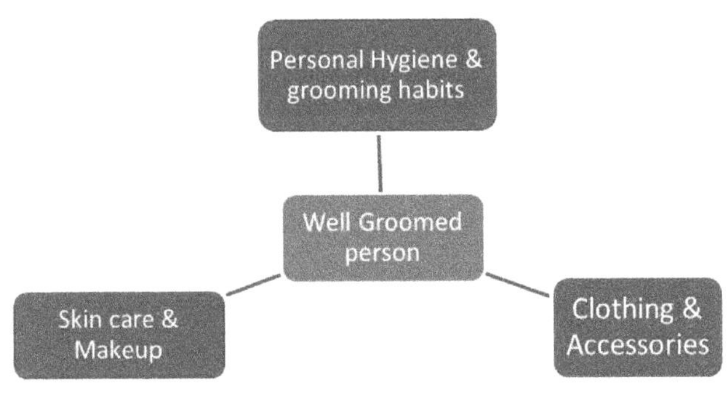


3 Pillars of personal grooming

Personal grooming habits are skills that help you boost your self-esteem and helps to maintain the overall hygiene of your body. Below listed are the areas you need to focus on to look well-groomed and how to maintain hygiene and rules of grooming are described in the following chapters.

## *10 Steps to become a Well-Groomed person*

***Here are the 10 steps you learn in the coming chapters: -***

1. Body care
2. Oral hygiene
3. Nose, Ears, Eyes Care & grooming
4. Feet & Legs Care & grooming
5. Hands & Nails Care & grooming
6. Body odour & bad Breath
7. Haircare
8. Skin & Face care
9. Makeup
10. Attire & Accessories

## *Personal Hygiene and Grooming Habits*

Personal grooming habits are skills that help you boost your self-esteem and confidence for striking personality and maintain the overall hygiene of your body. ***Personal grooming is essential to enhance your personal and professional appearance.***

Personal Hygiene means, maintaining a clean body and it is the first step to good grooming and good health. Every external part of the body demands a basic amount of attention on a regular basis. We need to follow some basic grooming routines daily.

**Hygiene** refers to the set of practices perceived by a community to be associated with the preservation of health and healthy living. While in modern medical sciences there is a set of standards of hygiene recommended for different situations, what is considered hygienic or not can vary between different cultures, genders, and various groups.

Society considers some regular hygienic practices as good habits, negligence of hygiene can be considered disgusting, disrespectful, or even threatening. Head lice, Bad Breath, Perspiration, body odour, infections, dandruff, ear wax, eye discharge, etc.... are examples of ***improper hygiene***.

Personal hygiene is taking care overall body, it includes practices like seeing a doctor, seeing a dentist, regular washing/bathing, and healthy eating.

***Personal grooming is an extension of personal hygiene as it pertains to the maintenance of a good personal and public appearance, which need not necessarily be hygienic.***

Personal Hygiene

## *Basic Personal hygiene Routine*

Body hygiene is achieved by using personal body hygiene products including soap, hair shampoo, toothbrushes, toothpaste, cotton swabs, antiperspirant, facial tissue, mouthwash, nail files, skin cleansers, toilet paper, and other such products.

***Here are steps for a basic personal hygiene routine: -***

- Overall health depends on personal hygiene. It's essential to bathe or shower at least once every day. If you're going out in the evening or in summer, it is better to take shower twice
- Take care of your oral hygiene by brushing your teeth at least twice.
- Wash hair regularly
- Wash hands multiple times a day
- Control body odour, foot odour and bad breath
- Take care of your skin Trim Finger and toenails and maintain good nail hygiene
- Comb hair neatly and take care of hair health
- Cover while coughing and sneezing

Let us discuss in detail how to maintain good grooming and hygiene of each body part to look well-groomed.

## *Body Care & Hygiene*

Each and every part of the body needs attention, needs to be maintained with good hygiene and care for a healthy body. Skincare for the body is necessary to keep you looking toned, fresh, and well-groomed. Just as the face needs regular deep cleansing and moisturising, so does your body. Use a natural bristle brush, loofah, body scrub or body mitt made for rubbing vigorously over the body to remove dead skin. Do this when the body is dry. Moisturise your body with a moisturizing lotion or coconut oil or virgin olive oil weekly, rubbed into your damp skin after a warm shower. Whenever you visit the bathroom, always wash your hands with hand soap as contaminated hands spread disease. Poor personal hygiene says that you don't care about yourself and the people around you

**Body Washes**

In order to maintain body hygiene, you have to certain body wash products. The best body washes will clean your skin without drying it out too. Always know your skin type, is your skin oily, dry, or sensitive.

Using soap for cleaning the body is another commonly used cleanser. However, soap bars are a little harsh on the skin because they remove the essential lipids and proteins which are responsible for keeping your skin supple.

The translucent bar soaps are made with glycerine (like Pears soap), it retains moisture in the skin and counteracts the drying effect of the soap. The creamy soaps available (like Dove soap) in the market for dry skin is helpful in retaining moisture. They are formulated with higher levels of lipids (fatty acids) like triglycerides, lanolin, and stearic acid. These ingredients form a protective film over your skin. Lastly, we have antibacterial bar soaps, which are not good for kids playing outdoors or sportsperson, but also for regular use for all body types. They contain ingredients like triclosan to restrict bacteria growth and body odour.

If you are facing any clogged pore issues on your body, you can also go for exfoliating body washes and soaps.

Please do note that sensitive skins may find exfoliation a bit rough.

It is always advisable to choose products free of harsh cleansers like sodium lauryl sulphate. However, please note that anything that foams and bubbles up is the result of sodium lauryl sulphate and hence most of the shampoos, body washes, face washes, soaps etc., have them.

You can check the ingredients list to find out. If you see ***sodium lauryl sulphate*** (otherwise known as SLS) and ***sodium laureate sulphate*** (SLES), both common but extremely harsh — cleaning agents. Also using authentic organic products will reduce the risk of harsh chemicals applied to your body.

## *Oral Hygiene*

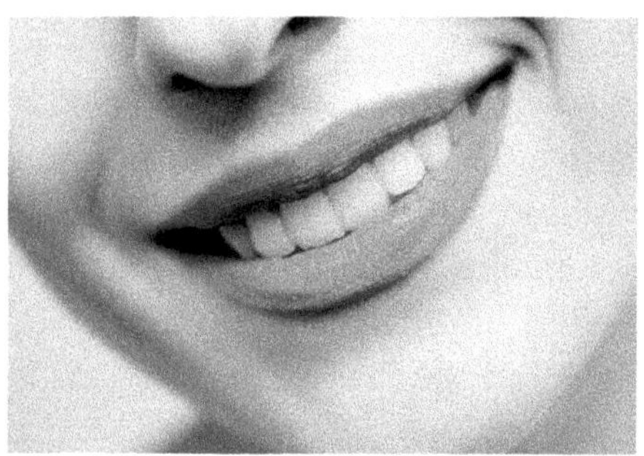

oral hygiene

Oral hygiene is all about taking care of the mouth, teeth, tongue, throat, and gums. Brush and floss your teeth twice a day. Remember to rinse your mouth after every meal. For those who smoke it is important you rinse your mouth after every smoke and use a mouth freshener. Brushing before going to bed is important. Pay attention to the tongue and the inner surface of teeth as well. Get your teeth cleaned professionally once every six months. If Teeth are coloured, go for Teeth Whitening. While brushing and flossing, pay attention to the food particles stuck in between the teeth and get rid of them. Brush should be rinsed well and left to dry after use and replace your toothbrush every three months once. In order to keep your teeth and gums healthy, brush your teeth from top to bottom, side to side and front and back of the teeth. Use mouth wash to avoid bad breath.

## ***Hands, Palms and Nail Hygiene and Grooming***

You use your hands all day long to express yourself. You can't do anything about the shape of your finger or the size of your hands, but you can enhance them through regular and simple grooming, including the maintenance of nails and cuticles and by using hand cream or lotion to keep the skin soft and smooth. ***Here are a few tips to take care of your hands and nails:-***

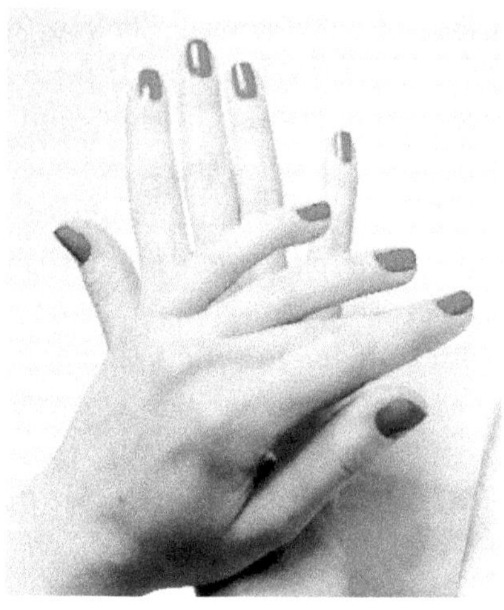

Hands & Nails care

**Hands Hygiene**

- Wash hands thoroughly with soap and water before and after every meal, after playing with pets, after smoking, after sneezing or coughing, after touching currency notes, after touching your ears or nose, and after visiting the toilet.
- Ensure that Soaping and rinsing should cover the areas between fingers, nails and back of the hand.
- Hands should be dried with a clean towel after washing, or you can use a hand dryer instead of a towel.
- The towel at the washstand must be washed and changed every day.

**Hands Grooming**

- Apply moisturizer/lotion/cream regularly to avoid dryness
- Get rid of dead cells by exfoliating
- Use Hand Sanitizer to keep your hand free from germs
- Remove hand hair if it is long, dark, and stubbly by waxing, shaving, hair removal creams temporarily or permanent hair removal with laser treatment

**Nail Hygiene**

- Clean your nails regularly.
- Maintain the shape of the nails, but clip nails short.
- Grow nails only if you can keep them clean.
- Brittle or discoloured nails show up deficiencies or disease conditions. So, maintain good health.

**Nail Grooming**

- Pamper your hands and nails once every two weeks with a manicure.
- Nails should be well shaped with a light to the medium colour application of nail polish.
- Nail polish on your nails should not be chipped.
- Extremely long nails or nails enamelled with very bright or dark shades of nail polish is not preferred in a professional environment.
- Use of mehndi on hands or any part of the body is not preferred in a professional environment.

**Manicure Steps**

Pamper your hands and nails once every 3 weeks with a manicure. You can do a manicure at home with easy steps.

A **manicure** is a beauty treatment for the fingernails and hands performed at home or in a salon. A manicure usually consists of filing and shaping the *free edge* of nails, pushing, and clipping any non-living tissue (but limited to the cuticle and hangnails), treatments with various liquids, massage of the hand, and the application of fingernail polish.

**How to apply nail polish?**

- Shake up your nail polish bottle before applying.
- Lightly start right above your cuticle, wiping your brush across to the end of your nail.
- Apply two coats of light nail polish, just don't get too close to the cuticle.
- Apply a top coat to make the nail polish lasts long and more shiny
- Also, make sure that you apply nail polish in just 2 – 3 vertical strokes.
- Repeat with all nails.

**Sweaty Palms Care**

***Sweaty palm*** is a condition that causes sweating in the palms of the hands. Excessive, uncontrollable sweating of the hands or palms is called palmar hyperhidrosis in medical terms. This medical condition is a very stressful, embarrassing, and confidence breaking problem. Sweaty palms are the reason for ruined paperwork to slippery handshakes and sweaty palms can negatively impact your social life, education, and career.

***Here are a few tips to take care of sweaty palms:*** -

- Don't Handshake with sweaty Palms.
- Use antiperspirants to avoid sweating a lot.

- Apply baby powder to your palms, the drying agents in the baby powder will help counteract mild sweating
- Combine equal parts baking soda and warm water and soak your hands for 25 minutes. The baking soda will help keep your hands dry for several hours
- Take medical help to permanently cure sweaty palms if it is severe.
- Clean your hands with a hand sanitiser, to prevent the growth of germs and it also prevents odour caused due to sweating.

## *Nose Hygiene & Grooming*

The nose is the prominent structure between the eyes. It is the entrance to the respiratory tract and contains the olfactory organ. It inhales air for respiration, helps to sense the smell, conditions the air by filtering, warming, and moistening it, and cleans itself of foreign debris extracted from inhalations.

Even though beauty is subjective, a straight nose is traditionally considered the most attractive nose shape. The nose has a large impact on overall facial harmony. If a nose is too small, the face can look flat and broad. If a nose is too large, the chin may appear less attractive, or other features may be overwhelmed. To bring the nose into harmony with other facial features, the permanent solution is rhinoplasty or nose surgery, or the temporary solution is makeup.

***Here are a few tips to take care of your Nose:*** -

- It is critical to **trim nose hair** if it starts peeping out.
- Keep Your Nose Clean if you are suffering from a cold.

- Blow your Nose quietly and discreetly, use tissue papers to blow and dispose of them after use.
- No Nose Picking.
- Blackheads and whiteheads appear on the surface of the nose and corners of the nose, exfoliate it regularly.

## *Eyebrows and Ears Care & Grooming*

Eyebrows are the most important feature on your face than eyes or nose. Your most recognisable defining feature is your brows, and they give a frame to your eyes. The practical purpose of eyebrows is to keep dust and dirt away from your eyes, brows help to define the emotional expression as well as facial recognition. if they are maintained nicely, your face looks neat.

***Here are a few tips to take care of your Eyebrows and Ears:***

-

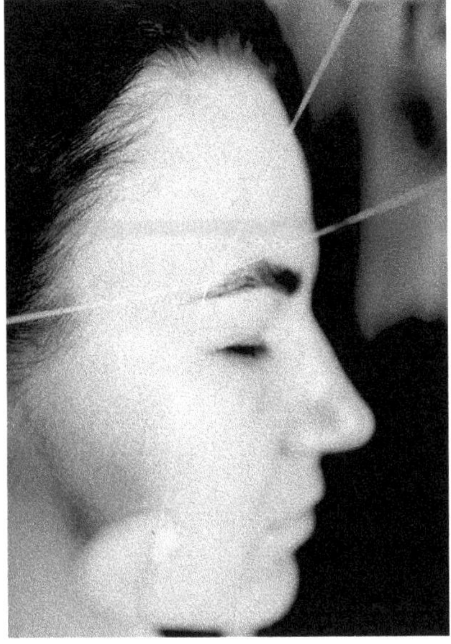

Eyebrows threading

- Your Eyebrows frame your eyes, the centre of our attention, so make sure they are well shaped and tidy.
- Trim eyebrows if they look bushy or if the eyebrows are connected in the middle.
- You can get your eyebrows trimmed with tweezers or a razor blade or by threading.
- It is critical to also **trim Ear hair** if it starts peeping out and outer ear hairs.
- Clean ears with water and soap.
- Clean only outer ear with Qtips
- Clean **ear wax** with care, as there are chances of hurting the eardrum.

## *Eyes Care*

The eyes are the most important sense organs in your body, it is a part of the central nervous system that reacts to visible light and allows us to see things, keep our balance and maintain circadian rhythm. The eye is considered a living optical device. It is very important to take care of the eyes by keeping them clean, protecting them from dust and infections and taking care of sensitive skin around the eyes. Beautiful eyes are considered attractive, so people tend to make them look attractive with eye makeup.

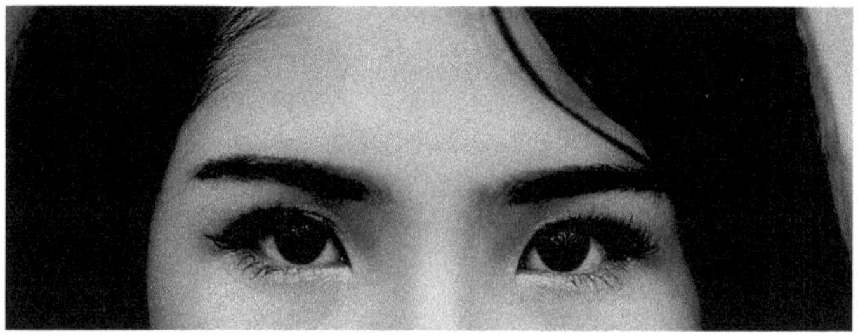

Eyes

***Here are a few tips to take care of your Eyes:*** -

- Wipe the Rheum (rheum or eye discharge or bloggers is thin mucus naturally discharged from the eyes, nose, or mouth during sleep) out of your eyes completely before going out.
- Wear sunglasses to protect your eyes from the Ultraviolet rays of the Sun.
- Wash Eyes with sterilized water or eye solution.
- Remove Eye makeup before sleeping.

- To prevent dark circles, give rest to your eyes and apply under eye cream as the skin under the eye is delicate and sensitive
- Always choose good products like eyeliner, kajal, mascara and eye shadow as eyes are very sensitive.

## *Sneezing, Yawning and Coughing Best practices*

Yawning is an involuntary action that forces us to inhale a deep breath and helps to boost oxygen to the brain.

Coughs are the body's way of clearing out your airway.

Sneezes, just like coughs also act as a protection for your body by forcefully ejecting airborne irritants such as pollen, dust, smoke, or odour along with germs like cold and flu viruses

This covid-19 period has taught the whole world the best practices to follow while sneezing and coughing.

The right way of Sneezing

***Here are a few tips to take care of while sneezing, coughing, and yawning: -***

- Don't Sneeze or cough or yawn without covering your nose or mouth.
- Cover your mouth with Tissue paper or handkerchief while sneezing or coughing and later dispose of the tissue paper. Sanitize your hands after disposing of the tissue paper to stop the spread of germs.
- Sneezing to your elbow is the best practice.
- Close Your Mouth while Yawning

## *Foot and Legs Care & Grooming*

Our Legs and feet are very important as we stand and move with the help of our legs. It is very important to take a few measures for pain-free clean, healthy, and hygienic foot.

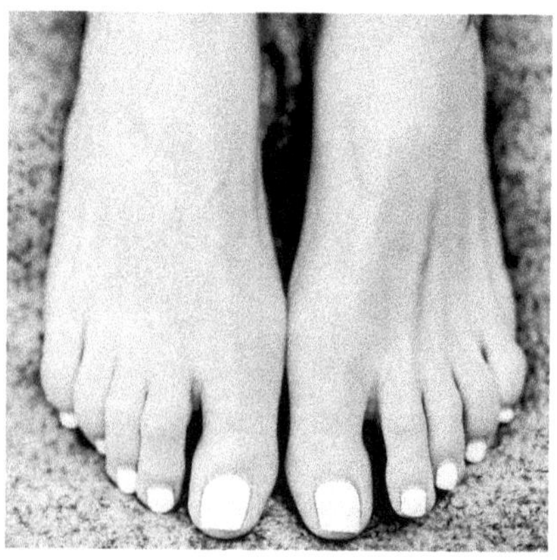

Feet care

***Here are a few tips to follow good foot hygiene & grooming...***

- Protect your feet when you go out. When you go to public pools or gyms or places where many people frequent, it becomes a breeding ground for fungi. Fungi can lead to infections. Hence always wear appropriate footwear to protect your feet.
- A very common measure, but an important one – keep feet clean and dry. Every day while bathing set aside three minutes for your feet. Clean and scrub the feet well with soap and water (in between the toes as well).
- Post cleaning, ensure that they are well dried before you put on your footwear. Any excess moisture will be prone to fungal infection.
- Use foot powder or antifungal powder to keep feet dry. If you are prone to sweaty feet Powder your feet before wearing socks.
- Those who wear shoes the whole day need to slip them off now and then as these air the socks and makes them less smelly. Wear cotton socks. Wear a clean pair of socks every day. Rotate your shoes, try not to wear the same shoe every day.
- Cut toenails keeping enough skin towards the nail bed. Cutting the nails too deep or into the edge can result in ingrown nails.
- Women must give breathing time in between nail paints. Continuous application of nail colour can lead to discolouration, yellowing of the nails, cracking, or crumbling of nails.
- Choose breathable footwear whenever possible. wear shoes made of leather to allow air to circulate and to

keep feet dry. Look for shoes made of mesh fabrics in case you have sweaty feet for maximum breathability.

- You need to look at the type of work you do before you choose footwear. Depending on the work, you can choose flat shoes, antislip shoes or shoes with reinforced toe caps. Wear high heels and pointed shoes only for special occasions. Wearing a high heel that's higher than 3 inches on a regular basis can damage your feet.
- Keep your legs clean and moisturize them with body lotion after a shower daily. Women can remove leg hair that is dark, long, and stubbly by shaving, waxing or laser treatment.

**PEDICURE**

A **pedicure** is a cosmetic treatment of the feet and toenails. Pedicures include care not only for the toenails; dead skin cells are rubbed off the bottom of the feet using a rough stone (often a pumice stone).

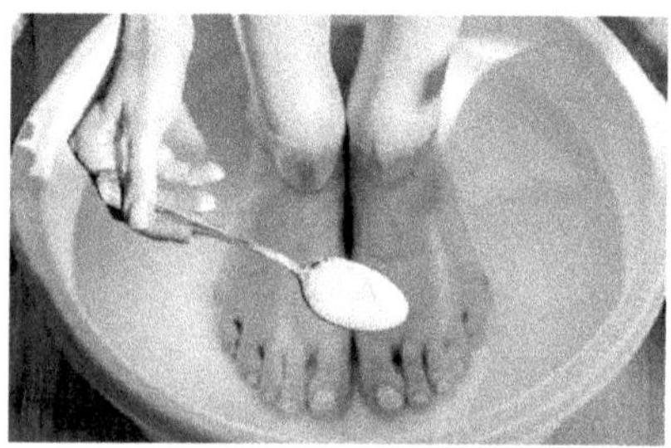

Foot Care

Pedicure is a simple treatment that includes foot soaking, foot scrubbing with a pumice stone or foot file, nail clipping, nail shaping, foot and calf massage, moisturizing, and nail polishing.

### Cracked Heels

- Cracked heels are caused when the skin around your heels splits apart. A mixture of dryness and pressure on feet lead to cracked heels, as the skin becomes unable to keep up moisture levels and ultimately becomes fragile, leading to breaks.
- To heal cracked heels, apply moisturizer to the feet daily, once in the morning and once at night before bed.
- After applying your lotion or cream, add a thin layer of a petroleum jelly-based product, like Vaseline, to seal moisture into your cracked feet.
- Shoes and sandals with open backs can cause cracked heels, make sure you protect the heels by wearing closed-back shoes along with socks instead of sandals

It is very important to practice the above-mentioned grooming habits to look well-groomed as hygiene is the basis for good grooming and to look polished.

# IV

# HAIR CARE& HAIR STYLES

"

***"I am my best self when I have super short hair. That's when I feel most like me and most confident"***

***--- Halle Berry***"

Hair is your "***Crowning Glory.***" Good hair grooming is vital for every woman. Keep your hair well maintained with the hair cut complimenting your features. Hair is one of the most important factor of your looks, how you carry them determines how healthy and hygienic and well maintained you are. The combination of hair texture, colour and style define healthy hair. Understand your hair type and use the products suitable for your hair type. Your hair may be Wavy, Curly or Straight and your hair might be dry or oily.

Hair Care

## *Haircare Tips*

**Here are a few tips to maintain your hair**: -

- Wash your hair a minimum of once a week, preferably 2 to 3 days once. Washing daily is not advisable as it dries your hair and removes natural oil out of the hair shaft.
- Scrub well and rinse properly when you wash.
- Oil the scalp, once a week, preferably an hour before hair wash or apply oil the night before and wash the next morning.
- Know your scalp and use hair care products accordingly.
- Take care of dandruff, use an anti-dandruff shampoo to get rid of dandruff.

- Maintain hair length and style at which you can take good care of hair.
- Brush your hair three to four times a day with a soft-bristled brush or a wide-toothed comb. Use long, slow, smooth strokes.
- Wash your brush and comb regularly to keep them clean
- Always go for haircuts at regular intervals between 68 weeks
- Preventing split ends gives your hair a well-groomed appearance. Trim your hair regularly to get rid of split and damaged ends.
- Untied hair should not cover any part of your face (e.g., eyes, forehead) and should still be neatly in place. Use hair clips, hair ribbons or hair bands to keep your hair in place.
- Don't Scratch your head, it is a real turn off.
- Don't overuse the blow dryer. It will dry out hair and make it weaker.
- Don't overuse hair spray. It traps dirt and makes hair stiff, so it breaks easily.
- Protect your hair with a scarf or hat if your hair is exposed to sun, wind or cold for long hours.

## Hair Care Routine

Here are a few basic steps to follow irrespective of hair type but use the products suitable for your hair type.

***The 5 Steps hair care routine for beautiful hair: -***

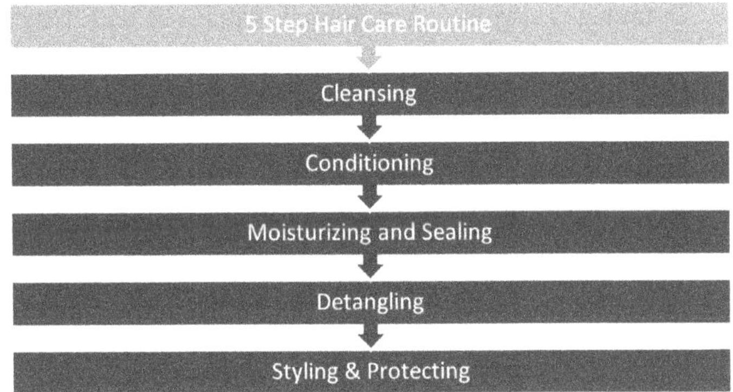


5- Step hair care routine

**Step 1 - Cleansing**

Cleansing is the first step in the hair care routine. You can use shampoo for removing dirt from your hair. Shampoo cleans hair without stripping hair of its natural oil. You can use regular or antidandruff shampoo based on your hair type and condition. Use a mild shampoo.

**Step 2 - Conditioning**

Conditioner moisturizes hair and makes them look shiny. Conditioner coats the hair strands to replenish the moisture that shampoo may have removed. You can use rinse-out, deep, or leave-in conditioner

**Step 3 - Moisturizing and Sealing**

To add further hydration to your hair you can follow two steps process moisturize and seal. The aim is to seal in moisture, not to lock in dryness, using a hydrating product and sealing oil. You can use Hair lotion or Oil for further protection from dryness and breakage and enhance your hair's natural oils to lock in moisture and to strengthen hair strands.

**Step 4 - Detangling**

Detangle is essential to stop the breakage of hair. Never comb on wet hair as it breaks easily. You can use a wide-toothed comb or brush or detangling spray or serum to detangle hair.

**Step 5 - Styling and Protecting**

For styling and protecting hair multiple products are available like hair mousse, hair spray, hair wax, Pomade, gel, dry shampoo, volumizer, shine serum etc... You can choose based on your need.

## *HAIRSTYLES FOR WORK*

Hair can make a lot of difference; you can look put together or messy depending on how you wear it.

***Here are a few tips to groom & style your hair***: -

- Hair should be always well-groomed with a neat appearance.
- Tie your hair in a neat hairstyle with hair pulled back from your face.
- Hair holding devices (clips, bands) should be plain and of natural colours.
- Get rid of frizz and split ends to look polished.
- If you have short hair (jawline length) then either leave it open or wear a hairband or wear a hair clip
- If you have shoulder-length hair, then tie a high pony or clip it
- If you have exceptionally long hair tie a neat braid or a classy bun or a ponytail
- Never leave your hair wet, always blow dry and comb neatly before leaving for work
- Trim your hair regularly

## *Best Hairstyles for Work*

Here are a few hairstyles that are preferred for work.

**PONYTAILS**

Ponytail

Ponytails look really polished when tied properly and is smooth and frizz-free. When your ponytail is tied low near your neck, it looks more professional. To ensure your hair looks very smart take a little section of the ponytail (from underneath the pony), wrap it around the elastic band as many times as you can to conceal the elastic and then use a bobby pin to fasten the little hair leftover (wrap the hair around the bobby and then through the middle) and then pin the bobby underneath the ponytail, push the bobby pin upwards and under so you can't see it.

**HALF UP AND DOWN HAIR**

One of the ideal hairstyles for the office. You can wear this style with a part or pull it straight back. Eliminate frizz before pinning it up. When the hair is neat and off the face, it still feels soft and feminine with hair still hanging loose.

**BUNS**

High Bun

When you are in hurry, then buns are great. Low bun looks more professional when done neater. Learn to do various kinds of low bun. You can also wear high bun if neatly done.

**BRAIDS**

Braids

French Braids or straight braids are considered as. If the braids are tight, without fly-away hairs escaping, then almost any braid is office-appropriate.

## ***Avoid these hairstyles for work as they look Unprofessional***

- Unbrushed long hair
- Messy Bun
- Pigtails
- Side Ponytail
- Too many Hair Clips
- Messy Waves

## *Managing & Grooming Unwanted Hair*

Facial hair, underarm hair, Upper lip hair, hair along chin line, bushy eyebrows, unibrow, nose hair, ear hair, legs and hands hair are considered as unwanted hair for women as it draws attention to that part and having them is considered as bad grooming. Removing unwanted hair is a vital grooming routine for women.

You can try waxing or shaving or hair removal creams for hands, underarm and legs hair removal, threading for eyebrows, upper lip, and chin hair. Waxing for facial hair removal. For permanent hair removal, you can opt laser treatment which is the safest and most effective solution for hair removal. Getting rid of unwanted hair from the body makes you look more attractive and presentable without any distraction in your appearance.

“***“A woman who cuts her hair is about to change her life”***

***--- Coco Chanel***”

# V

# UNDERSTANDING & MANAGING BODY ODOUR

*"As the sense of smell is so intimately connected with that of taste, it is not surprising that an excessively bad odour should excite retching or vomiting in some persons"*
*--- Charles Darwin*

In previous chapters, you understood about hygiene, the importance of grooming habits and hair care. In this chapter, you are going learn about body odour which is a result of mainly bad grooming habits and how to prevent bad odours with a proper grooming routine.

## *Definition of Body Odour*

**Body odour** is an unpleasant smell of our bodies and is the result of bacterial activity.

**Body odour** is a perceived unpleasant smell our bodies can give off when bacteria that live on the skin break down sweat into acids, it is the result of bacteria breaking down protein into certain acids.

**Our body has two different sweat glands** namely eccrine and apocrine glands. Eccrine glands are all over your body and produce watery sweat to keep your body cool. Apocrine glands are located where hair follicles are most concentrated (scalp, armpit, and groin), and the sweat is waxy and fatty from the lipids they secrete. The more hair you have, the more surface area bacteria get to cling to, which keeps the smell pungent.

Types of Body Odour

## *Types of Body odour*

- Underarm Odour
- Feet Odour
- Bad Breath or Halitosis
- Flatulence

## *Underarm Odour*

Underarm odour is one of the body odours which is prominent and most of us face it every day. If you have dressed well, your makeup, your clothes and your hair are perfect but if you smell bad, it gives out a negative impression, so addressing this issue is of utmost importance to look well-groomed.

**Causes of the body (mainly Underarm) Odour**

There are many reasons for body odour, below I have mentioned a few causes of body odour. Identifying the reason why you have body odour is the first step and by following the tips provided, you can get rid of or minimize body odour.

***Here are a few causes for body odour***: -

- Excessive Sweat in the armpit and other body parts is the cause of body odour.
- Medications taken for certain health conditions cause body odour.
- Bad personal Hygiene and not following the grooming habits mentioned earlier is the main cause for body odour.

- Hormonal Imbalance is also one of the causes.
- Food affects your body odour
- Stress produces more sweat and in turn, causes body odour.
- Wearing Synthetic fabrics cause body odour as these fabrics won't absorb sweat.
- Skin issues like fungal or bacterial infections are one of the causes of body odour.

**Prevention of Body Odour (mainly Underarm)**

By following the tips mentioned below regularly you can reduce or get rid of body odour.

Roll-on Deodorant

***Here are a few tips to prevent body odour: -***

- Taking 2 baths a day, with liberal lathering and change of clothes in close contact with the body should take care of the problem. Always take bath after a workout as more sweat is released from the body during the workout.

- You can use talcum powder of the nonmedicated kind under the armpits.
- Deodorants or antiperspirants could be used if you perspire more underarm.
- In hot weather, wear light-coloured, cotton clothing and socks. This will absorb less heat and **sweat stains** will be less visible as cotton absorbs sweat.
- The armpits should always be trimmed. The more hair you have, the more surface area bacteria get to cling to, which keeps the smell pungent.
- Use roll-on deodorant or deo spray to curb the bad smell that is caused by sweating. You can use roll-on antiperspirant deodorant.
- Use **Perfume** at your pulse points (wrist, behind ears, throat). Don't apply perfume underarm, if applied it mixes with sweat and produces a bad smell.
- Watch your diet and habits and care accordingly. Eating spicy food, onion, garlic, fish, drinking alcohol causes body odour.
- Drink more water at least 68 glasses per day as water flush out toxins from the body

## *Bad Breath Causes and Prevention*

In the previous chapter, while learning about grooming habits, you learnt about the importance of oral hygiene and how to take care of your teeth, tongue, and mouth. If the hygiene routine is not followed you end up with bad breath. Bad breath is a result of bad oral hygiene.

Bad breath

**Causes of Bad Breath**
***Here are a few causes for Bad breath:*** -

- Any food trapped on your teeth, particularly between the teeth is broken down by bacteria, which causes bad **breath**.
- Poor Dental Hygiene and Gum disease causes bad breath
- If you have any health problems like Sore throat, cold, sinus infections, diabetes, you will have bad breath.
- If your mouth is Dry and if you keep your mouth closed for a long time, your breath smells.
- Eating Strongly flavoured food like onion, garlic, fish or drinking coffee or tea
- Not maintaining the hygiene of Dentures or braces
- Drinking Alcohol, Smoking and Chewing Tobacco also causes bad breath.

**Prevention of Bad Breath**

***Here are a few tips to prevent Bad Breath: -***

- Brushing and flossing teeth and cleaning the tongue helps to get rid of bad breath, at least in the short term (proper dental hygiene).
- Mouthwash may temporarily mask bad breath and can help with oral hygiene.
- Chewing sugarless gum or sucking on sugar-free mints may temporarily mask bad breath odour.
- Chewing herbs like mint leaves or tulsi (Basil) leaves and chewing cardamom helps.
- Every time after smoking rinse your mouth with mouthwash and use mouth freshener like mint, titbits etc...
- Drink plenty of water to avoid a dry mouth and gargle with warm salt water to flush out bacteria causing bad breath.

## *Foot Odour (Stinky feet) causes and prevention*

Foot odour happens when the bacteria living on your feet skin and in your shoes eat sweat. This produces an acid byproduct that smells unpleasant, says podiatrist ***Joy Rowland.***

Smelly feet

**Causes of foot Odour**

***Here are a few causes for Foot odour:*** -

- Poor Personal Hygiene.
- Overactive Sweat glands. Bacteria on the skin breaking down sweat produces an unpleasant smell
- Hormonal Changes and Stress
- Fungal Infections or bacterial infections.
- Wearing the same Shoes daily without letting them dry.
- Not changing socks every day

**Prevention of foot Odour or Caring Stinky feet**

- Give your feet a good scrub when having a bath.
- Soak your feet in a mixture of vinegar and water or Epsom salt and water for cleaning
- Keep your feet dry. Dry after feet after cleaning, dry between toes also. An unpleasant odour comes from

moisture, so always keep your feet, shoes and socks dry.

- Keep toenails clipped and go for a pedicure at least once in 3 weeks.
- Those who wear shoes always need to slip them off now and then. This airs the socks slightly and makes them less smelly.
- Wear cotton socks. Wear a clean pair every day.
- Powder your feet before wearing socks. You can use talcum powder or foot antiperspirant.
- Rotate your Shoes do not wear the same shoe every day.

## *Flatulence (Fart or Gas) causes and prevention*

Flatulence is one of the body's deadly by-products is produced by the food people eat and the gas in one's intestine.

Farting in public can be really embarrassing so it can be helpful to understand the underlying causes of farting and how to avoid it in public.

**Causes of Flatulence**

- Lactose (Milk) Sensitivity.
- Swallowing excess air due to rushed eating or drinking or chewing gum or drinking soda.
- The gas diffuses into our intestines from our bloodstream.
- Chemical reactions involved in digestion.
- Bacterial fermentation of undigested foods, particularly certain indigestible carbohydrates, and fibres in the large intestine.
- Eating food like Beans, Sprouts, Broccoli, potatoes etc ...

## Prevention of Flatulence

- Try peppermint tea or eat mint leaves.
- It is important to drink enough water.
- Take healthy food rich in fibre and maintain a healthy lifestyle.
- Fennel Seeds tea.
- Using Ginger, caraway seeds, papaya, and pineapple help.

***Do you know?*** According to the Study, your image is affected due to Body odour is 59%, due to Bad Breath is 37%, Appearance due to facial, ear & nasal hair is 4%, Dirty ears - 1% and 83 % have had its impact on their social lives. Body odour can affect Self-confidence and body image too. So, it is necessary to cultivate good grooming habits.

***"“Body odour is the window to the soul”***
***---- David Byrne"***

# VI

# THE SECRET OF SKIN CARE

***"“Skin Care is like dieting. You have to invest time and effort. There is no instant miracle cure”***
***--- Karen Grant"***

Skin is the largest organ of your body, and it plays an important role in your overall health, and the focus needs to be on its protection. Skin is your true reflection and is the first source to identify serious diseases e.g., Diabetes, Hepatitis, or Cancer. Skin also reflects emotions: Nervous or frightened expressions, you break out in cold sweat, or your hair may stand on end, or you may get Goosebumps. Your skin also changes colour. Psychologists have agreed that skin quality is a primary factor in the development of self-esteem. Considering what all it does, your skin deserves better attention.

Taking care of your skin is extremely important as you age, your skin becomes drier and more wrinkled. You can look young for a long time if you take care of your skin without the need for surgeries or procedures. The largest organ in your body is the skin. It covers an area of around twenty square feet. Its several purposes are to protect the body from microbes, to assist in the regulation of body temperature, and for sensations of cold, heat, and touch. It consists of three layers: the Epidermis, Dermis and Hypodermis. The Epidermis is the outer layer of skin, that creates the skin tone and provides a barrier it is waterproof. The number of layers of skin depends on the part of the body. The skin underneath the eyelids is the thinnest and the skin at the bottom of the feet is thicker. The thickness of the skin depends on age and gender as well. For most people, the skin thins as we age.

The skin sheds and renews itself every four or five weeks. The old cells become dust and the skin renews itself. You shed almost two pounds of dead skin cells each year. Once the new cells reach the surface, they look fresh. They do not show signs of wear and tear from the environment. The process of skin renewal improves the appearance and makes the skin look more healthy

The core cells for colour are called melanocyte cells. The melanocyte cells make pigment, also called melanin, which gives colour to the hair and skin. As we understood it is extremely important to take care of our skin, let us learn how to care for and groom our skin.

### *Basic Skin Care Routine: -*

- Soap and water are essential for keeping the skin clean. A good bath once or twice a day is recommended for good hygiene.

- Those who engage in active sports or work out and sweat a lot should take shower after the activity.
- Drying with a clean towel is important after bath.
- Avoid sharing soaps and towels.
- Apply cream or body lotion to prevent skin from becoming dry.

## *Types of Skin*

There are 5 types of skin we can see in human beings( each skin type is explained in the makeup chapter)

- Normal Skin
- Oily Skin
- Dry Skin
- Combination Skin
- Sensitive Skin

## *8 Step Skin Care Routine for Young, Healthy and Radiant skin*

***Here are the 8 Steps of Skincare Routine for Beautiful Skin: -***

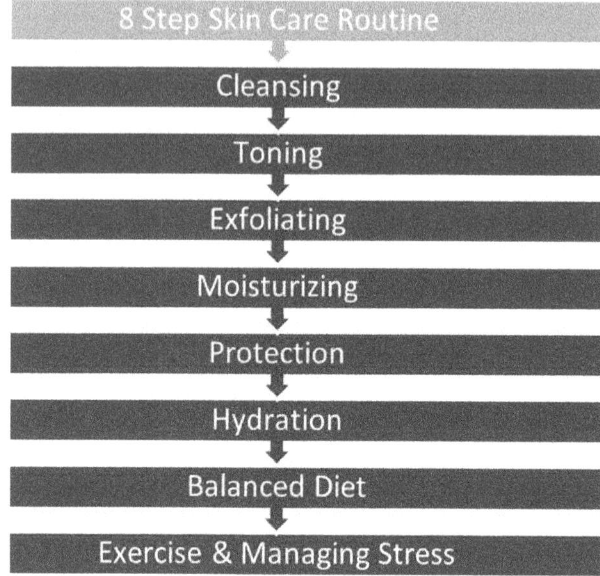


skincare steps

Following these steps consistently leads to healthier and better-looking skin.

***Here is the description for all the 8 steps: -***

**Step 1- Cleansing**

The cleansing process removes the dead skins cells, impurities, excess oil, dirt, bacteria, and other things that can be harmful. The cleansing process can also dry the skin out because it also removes the oils from the skin. Liquid or gel cleansers in the form of face wash or cleansing gels are better for the skin than bar soaps because they don't dry out the skin. They normally contain moisturizers that can add moisture back to the skin and combat the drying out process. Some skin cleansers contain Vitamin E, which aids in the restoration of moisture and elasticity. Cleaning should be a daily part of your skin regime at least twice with products suitable for your skin type.

**Step 2- Toning**

Toning removes final traces of makeup, leaves the skin tighter with less noticeable pores. Toning calms, soothes, and balances the skin's PH. Toning should be twice daily, once in the morning and once before bed.

**Step 3- Moisturizing**

When your skin is dry, it gets damaged and can crack. Keeping your skin moisturized will help it remain pliable and better looking. It will be harder for your skin to wrinkle because it won't be dehydrated and will be able to function properly. Apply moisturizing lotion or petroleum jelly or olive oil as soon as you come out of the shower, as it locks the moisture and keeps skin hydrated. Moisturizing should be twice daily.

**Step 4- Exfoliation and Scrubs**

Get rid of the dead skin cells by scrubbing, so that new cells come to the surface. When you exfoliate, dead skins cells are washed away, the pores open and as the pores tighten back after toning, the result is smoother skin. The new skin cells have not been damaged by the wind and the sun, as a result, skin looks fresh and radiant. Exfoliation is recommended once a week.

**Step 5- Sun Protection**

Sunscreen should be a daily part of your skin regime. It provides protection to every age group, gender, and unique skin type. Applying Sunscreen on daily basis lessens the chances of developing skin cancer, skin damage and other skin concerns during adulthood. It acts as a shield that protects your skin from harmful UVA and UVB rays. Sunscreen reduces the chances of developing wrinkles and age spots. It enhances skin health.

Exposure to ultraviolet rays for a long time cause damage to the fibres in the skin called elastin. Once elastin begins to break down, the skin also begins to lose its elasticity and will start to sag and stretch, losing its ability to bounce back to how it was before.

To provide your skin with optimum protection from UVA and UVB rays, your sunscreen should have an SPF of 15 or higher and should be broad-spectrum.

Buy a broad-spectrum sunscreen lotion or gel which is non-comedogenic and hypoallergenic. The sunscreen protects your skin from Ultraviolet rays and safeguards your skin from rashes, tanning, acne, sunburns and clogged pores.

Use Sunscreen with **SPF 15-30** during Winter and with **SPF 30-50** during Summer. If the sunscreen is waterproof, it should have a minimum SPF of 30

Ensure you always apply sunscreen 30 minutes before going outdoors. You can do research and find yourself the best suitable sunscreen for your skin type.

**Step 6- Hydration**

Drink lots of water to keep yourself hydrated, at least 6-8 glasses. When you are dehydrated, your skin becomes loose, saggy, starts peeling and looking dull. If you stay hydrated skin will look more radiant and beautiful. Drinking more water balances PH value thereby giving you healthy skin. Water flushes out the toxins in your body. By drinking more water, you won't suffer from acne, pimples, and clogged pores. In addition, hydration can really reduce the signs of ageing by maintaining the elasticity of the skin. It reduces wrinkles and fine lines and maintains overall skin health. Water is essential for making your body function well and works to add moisture back into your skin.

**Step 7- Balanced Diet**

Eating a healthy balanced diet prevent the formation of wrinkles. Eat food rich in antioxidants like fruits and vegetables. People who eat a balanced diet have better skin because their body is getting all the nutrients their skin needs. A Diet rich in vitamin C and E helps the immune system and produces more collagen, as a result, fewer wrinkles, softer skin and more elastic.

**Step 8- Exercises and Stress**

Doing Exercises regularly reduces your stress levels, for example, Yoga, cycling, taking walks, listening to soothing music, giving yourself more time, and getting enough sleep. Meditation helps you to keep your mind peaceful and reduces stress levels. Ensure you get a good sleep of 7 to 8 hours; it relaxes and rejuvenates your body.

## *Anti-Ageing Skin care*

Following these tips helps to delay the early ageing of the skin.

- Use good night creams after CTM (cleansing, toning, and moisturizing) process.
- Use a good cleanser or a makeup remover for removing makeup.
- Consume Vitamin/skin supplements and calcium once you cross 25 years of age.
- Wash your face preferably with normal water or lukewarm water to avoid open pores.
- Skin glows with proper sleep, make sure that you sleep for at least 8 hrs. and avoid stress.
- People with wrinkles and loose skin can consult dermatologists for skin treatments

If you want to look younger and have healthier skin, follow the above rules for Skincare. By following these steps, you can minimise the progression of ageing and keep the skin healthier, fresher, smoother and more radiant.

> “ ***“Be good to your skin. You’ll wear it every day for the rest of your life.”***
> ***– Renee Rouleau***
> ”

# VII

# MAKEUP: YOUR WAY TO SUCCESS

> ***"Makeup is not a mask that covers up your beauty; it's a weapon that helps you express who you are from the inside."***
> ***- Michelle Phan.***

In the previous chapter, you learned everything about personal grooming and Personal hygiene habits. In this chapter, we learn about the importance of makeup and makeup tips for work. Makeup is like the finishing touch to appear well-groomed. Even though many women don't use makeup daily or use it very little, still makeup is certainly a big part of a well-groomed impression. In earlier chapters, you learnt about first impressions and how appearance matters. You must make sure to create the right impression by completing your work outfit with appropriate makeup and hairdo. When you are working, you represent your business or the company you work for, so appearance is important.

Here I am sharing office makeup tips that you can implement in a few minutes to look polished and professional. In the previous chapter, we have learnt about the Skincare routine, in this chapter, we focus only on facial skin. Facial Skin is more sensitive than the skin in other parts of the body. As the face skin is always exposed, special care needs to be taken every day with proper hygiene and using suitable products by considering your skin type.

## *Definition & Importance of makeup*

***Makeup*** is defined as the way someone or something is put together or composed. *Cosmetics.* or coloured substances are used on your face to improve or change your appearance is called makeup

In 1920 **Max Factor** created the first make-up line and coined the word calling this new range **'Society Make-up'.**

Archaeological evidence of cosmetics dates back at least from ancient Egypt and Greece. According to one source, Egyptians were using castor oil as a protective balm and olive oil and rose water were used by Romans.

*Makeup is about enhancing and intensifying your beauty, rather than copying someone else's look. It is not one look fits all, but need to consider your personality, face shape and lifestyle. Beauty is often perceived as one of the most pleasant aspects of life. When you look at someone, the first thing you notice is their skin, lips, and eyes. Smooth Glowing Skin and flush cheeks portray health and youth. Health and beauty go hand to hand. Cosmetics are used by women of all ages to enhance their appearance. A younger woman wears makeup to boost their confidence and an older woman wears it to look young. Our perception of ourselves comes from our health and mood.*

*Wearing makeup gives confidence and you feel good about yourself. Even a small amount of makeup adds to a well-groomed look and statistics prove that women who wear makeup earn more than those who don't!*

## Why Wear Makeup?

Each person has different reasons and benefits for wearing makeup. Here are the reasons for wearing makeup:-

- Applying makeup is a feel-good factor for most of us.
- Makeup helps in Countering facial variations like accentuating your good features and hiding imperfections.
- Makeup helps in Concealing scars/marks, minimizing pores, and uneven patches. Covers blemishes and acne marks.
- Makeup Boosts confidence.
- It gives you a lift when you are feeling low. Makeup is not only about physical enhancement but is also a psychological enhancement
- Makeup gets you positive attention in public and helps to look professional and polished
- Makeup transforms someone's face and makes them look younger.
- Makeup adds hue, value, intensity contrast on the face – Colour contrast

## Preparing Skin before Makeup

- **Skin type:** Know your skin type, your skin may be Normal Skin, Dry Skin, Oily Skin, Combination Skin or Sensitive Skin. Based on the skin type use the products specified for that skin type (check below to know how to identify your skin type).

*For oily skin, use more powder base make-up, for dry skin, use a good moisturizer base and for combination skin, use water-based make-up, for sensitive consult doctor and use the recommended products*

- **Facial hair:** Bleaching/waxing is recommended in case they are thick, dark, and prominent.
- **Upper lip:** prominent hair to be removed as it would spoil the entire look.
- **Eyebrows:** Should be shaped properly by removing extra hair and should look neat as eyebrows give a frame to your face.
- **Skincare**: Follow the CTM process for good skin along with exfoliation (for more details refer to the Skincare chapter).

***The basic skincare routine includes four steps, popularly known as CTMP*** *(description in Skincare chapter)*

- Cleansing
- Toning
- Moisturizing
- Protection

## *How to identify your Skin Type?*

Knowing skin type is essential to take good care of the skin and to choose cosmetics suitable for skin type.

**Steps to evaluate your skin type-**

- Cut tissue paper or brown paper into 2-inch squares.
- Label 5 squares: forehead, nose, chin, left cheek and right cheek.
- Wash your face with mild soap and wait for 2 hours.
- Pull your hair back with a band.
- Press the paper squares on your skin according to the label.
- Then check the paper from each area of your face to see the excess oil.
- On dry areas, the paper may not stick whereas it may perfectly stick on the oily/greasy area leaving a mark on the paper.
- If the paper sticks well on all areas, you have oily skin.
- If the paper slips off from all areas, consider your skin to be dry.
- If the paper sticks to some parts and slips off from other areas, you have combination skin.

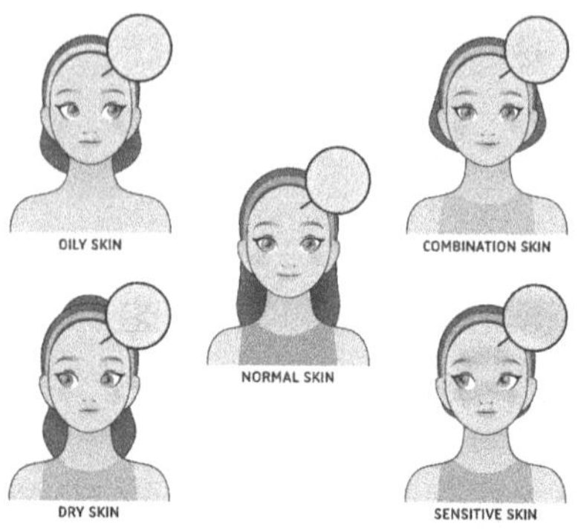


Skin types

## *Types of Makeup*

Makeup is decided based on the occasion for which you are wearing makeup. Makeup is different if you are attending a Job interview or if you are going to a party, or if you are an actor.

***The two main types of makeup are-***

- **Natural Look / No Make-up Look / Nude Makeup Look:**

Natural makeup look

This makeup is applied during Day time. It gives natural look and could be applied for Formal occasions, business, meetings, presentations, etc.

- **Glamour Look / Fashion Look / Evening look**

Glamour look

Glamour look is suitable for Evening time and this look is applied for evening semi-formal to informal party occasions like business dinner, weddings etc.

## *Office Wear Make Up Tips*

The main aspect of Office wear makeup is, it should be of a flawless complexion and should stay for a long time regardless of bad weather.

- Makeup should be natural looking
- It should be of low maintenance and easy to apply.
- It should enhance your natural beauty and should not alter your features
- It should not be distracting
- Makeup should be light, subtle, and carefully applied Light to medium shades.
- Avoid too glossy and shimmering products for office
- Apply medium to light lip colours like Pinks, peaches, and russets.
- Eye makeup should look natural, a light application of mascara, a light shade of eye shadow and eyeliner is good to go.
- Nail polish and lip colour should not be too trendy or bright. Stay away from extremely dark, bright reds and fluorescent colours.
- Hair colour should not be more than one or two shades darker or lighter than your natural hair colour. Unnatural colours (burgundy, green, etc.) must be avoided.

- Apply mild fragrance and deodorant to smell fresh and avoid body odour.

**Makeup Steps**

Always while doing makeup keep in mind Less is more and keep it fresh and simple.

***Here are the 8 steps of basic makeup application:-***

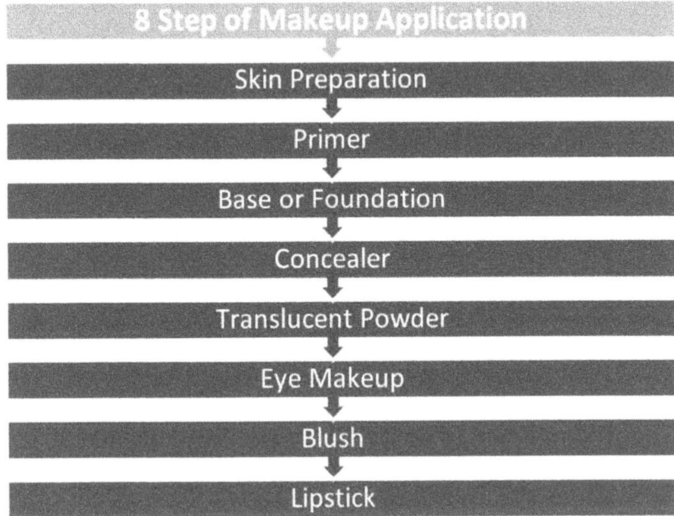


Makeup Steps

**Step 1: Skin Preparation**

As explained above follow CTMP (cleansing, toning, moisturizing and sun protection) skincare steps. This is the first step that prepares skin for makeup.

**Step 2: Primer**

It gives a smooth base to the skin and most makeup products blend smoothly when you apply primer on the skin. It also minimizes pores.

**Step 3: Base or Foundation**

Foundation is a product that evens out the complexion and covers imperfections. Foundation is like a building block for makeup. Foundation should be selected in such a way that it matches the skin colour. There are many types of foundation available in the market like cream foundation, liquid foundation, powder foundation or tinted moisturizers like BB cream.

**Step 4: Concealer**

Concealer is slightly thicker than foundation and lighter than foundation. It not only conceals the pigmentation but also balances the uneven colouration/patches.

**Step 5: Translucent Powder**

It sets makeup, evens out skin tone and softens the appearance by eliminating the shine. The translucent powder comes in various colours, pick up the one that matches your skin tone.

**Step 6: Eye Makeup**

Keep your eye makeup simple. The best options for eye makeup are matte eyeshadows in neutral shades like browns, taupe, or bronze along with eyeliner is good for office wear. Brows frame the eyes, don't forget to fill the eyebrows. You can use an eyebrow pencil, powder, or brow gel.

**Step 7: Blush**

Blush is all about adding colour. A little blush can brighten your complexion and make you look fresh Depending on how much makeup you're wearing, or even the time of year, you might benefit from a pop of colour to your cheeks. Apply blush to the apples of your cheeks

**Step 8: Lipstick**

A little lip colour looks smart and professional. Lip Makeup comprises lipstick, lip liner & lip gloss. Avoid fun colours like orange and hot pink. For a daily look, you can either apply a nude lip pencil and a gloss, choose a creamy lipstick in a dark pinkish nude hue. Neutral pinks and soft subtle corals are the best choices for your typical office day.

Follow these make-up steps, for a simple and professional look. Makeup is the first thing people notices, so keep it simple and fresh.

***"“MAKEUP IS A WAY FOR A WOMAN TO LOOK AND FEEL LIKE HERSELF, ONLY PRETTIER AND MORE CONFIDENT”***

***– Bobbi Brown"***

# VIII

# THE ART OF DRESSING (ATTIRE)

> ***"Dress shabbily and they remember the dress; dress impeccably and they remember the woman."***
> ***—Coco Chanel***

In previous chapters, you learnt about the importance of Personal grooming habits, personal hygiene, and makeup and how to apply it in our lives. In this chapter, you are learning about one of the important aspects of Appearance that is clothing and how we can use this resource to create powerful impressions and we shall discuss how grooming can be used by us to express ourselves better in different scenarios.

## *Importance of Attire*

As a person living and working in a highly competitive society, you must recognize and identify the impact of your appearance (your visual resume) as it communicates first to you and then to others. **Judith Rasbandsays what you wear(clothing) and the way you look (Grooming) affects**:

- the way you **think**,
- the way you **feel**,
- the way you act or **behave**, and then
- the way others **react or respond** to you.

It is important to like what you wear and the way you look, and it is more important to understand why or why not, specifically how this affects you, your life, your goals achievement, and others. Your professional appearance needs to support your professional accomplishments, which is why looking competent and confident is incredibly important.

Your professional image should not be underestimated, especially if you're planning to advance in your career and achieve your goals. As a career woman, the thought and care you put into your image should not be limited to the outfits you choose for your business meetings or interviews but should reflect in every aspect that ties together the whole ensemble. The most important fact is that your appearance influences the opinions of everyone around you. Finally, appearances do count, not only in first impressions but also in ongoing interactions. Your professionalism, intelligence and the trust, people form in you is mainly due to your appearance. Overall appearance includes your Clothing, Grooming, Hygiene, Makeup,

Accessories, Body language and Etiquette.

Different scenarios need different types of grooming. The type of grooming we maintain can give a formal, informal, or casual vibe in the respective environment. Let us look at different levels of formality and the way we need to groom ourselves for it. It includes some options for clothes and accessories. It helps us to understand what a particular type of dress code communicates to the perceiver.

Clothes also have different categories based on the occasion: Formal, casual, semi-formal etc., however earlier there was no measuring tool to define how formal is formal or how casual is casual.

***Judith Rasband*** (AICI CIM), who is one of the top Image Management Consultants worldwide created the **Style Scale® which is internationally accepted**.

The Style Scale®, dress code, is a solution to business casual issues of dressing, the biggest benefit of this tool is that it has defined guidelines to know how formal is formal and how casual is casual and what comes in between in exact terms with different degrees of going up the scale or below the scale. Style Scale is an easy reference tool to align perceived messages with the clothes you wear in different situations of life.

The Style Scale accurately identifies **four levels of dressing** to meet all personal, professional, and social needs.

## *4 Levels of Dressing*

- Tailored (Formals)
- Softly tailored (Business Casuals)

- Casual tailored (Business Casuals)
- Untailored (Casuals)

## *Tailored levelor Business Formals*

This is the most formal dress code. A woman at a tailored level communicates professionalism and a sense of authority. Her outfit says that she is focused, sharp, capable, credible, persuasive, and knowledgeable. People around her treat her with respect as she displays an official image. This is a more formal dress code as compared to the other three levels.

Business formals

This dress code is often suggested for daytime office wear at executive levels, top management levels front office executives, for presentations, high profile sales meetings and semi-formal events like work lunches, delegate meets and conferences. The idea behind this dress code is to wear something that is essentially a dressed-up version of your best office wear. However, one must keep in mind that the third layer and bottom should match.

**Examples**- Matched Pantsuit, blazer and skirt, dress, and blazer. With reference to Indian wear kurta and jacket with straight-cut pants, saree with matching jacket.

## *Softly tailored level*

This is the less formal dress code compared to the previous level and is also called business casuals. A woman in business casual attire is influential, capable, and more accessible. Her outfit says that she is trustworthy, dependable, capable of managing others, receptive to others and consistent.

BUSINESS CASUALS

This dress code is suggested for office wear in companies where the dress code is not very formal, employees wear business casuals for conferences, delegate meetings, presentations, team meetings, etc

**Examples** - Any third layer that goes well with a nice buttoned-up shirt and trousers is accepted. With reference to Indian wear, an unmatched blazer or jacket can be worn on the Saree. If it is a Kurta, then it can be combined with straight-cut pants and heels with a formal blazer or a jacket.

### *Casual tailored level*

This level of dress code is more casual than formal and comes under business casuals in a more relaxed way. A woman in casual tailored attire is perceived as Approachable, Flexible, Cooperative and Relaxed compared to formal or business casual attire.

casually tailored

This dress code is suitable for back-office work, preparatory meetings, projects, rural sales calls, regular office wear for entry-level jobs, for social occasions where you are out with friends, shopping, or movies.

A third layer is not necessary for this dress code, you can wear a vest or sweater as the third layer and the shirt must have a collar.

**Examples** - You can wear a Shirt/blouse collar along with Pants/skirts. With reference to Indian wear, you can wear crisp ironed Kurtas with a collar along with straight pants or palazzos. Also, you can wear Sarees with collared blouses or saree with blouse and vest.

## *Untailored level*

This level of dress code is casual wear. A woman in an Untailored attire is perceived as Agreeable, Available, Casual, easy-going and temporary. It is functional, comfortable, Stylish, and least in formality and conveys temporary vibes compared to other dress codes.

casuals

Casual wear is unstructured and hence you can mix and match any colour or any casual style. It all depends on your functional requirement and the occasion.

This dress code is suitable for weekends, sports activities, physical labour, offsite retreat, recreational activities, for social occasions where you are hanging out with friends, parties, holidaying, shopping, movies or at-home wear. It essentially depends on your social environment

**Examples** – Sportswear, Jeans, Shorts. With reference to Indian wear, you can wear Kurtas, short tops, with leggings, jeans, or palazzos.

## *Corporate Dressing Tips*

- Corporate dressing refers to the art of dressing formally and correctly.
- Corporate dressing helps an individual to dress according to her work profile and organization culture which helps an individual to make a mark of her own in the first meeting itself.
- Corporate dressing along with personal grooming help you create a presence that exudes professionalism, leadership, confidence, and elegance.
- Dressing formally not only reflects your image but also the organization you represent.
- Do not wear something which will make you feel the odd one out at the workplace. Dressing sensibly makes you feel confident throughout the day.
- Dress something suitable for your body type, body shape and personal colours. Corporate dressing helps you get

noticed, hence wear something appropriate and authentic to the occasion and the role and goals.

- A formally dressed person is considered a mature professional and a casually dressed person is often not treated as a serious sincere employee
- Always wear Clean and Ironed Clothes. For formal occasions choose the outfit as suggested under tailored, softly tailored, and casual tailored levels of dressing.
- Wear Solid colours and small prints preferably geometric prints for work and avoid ill-fitting, sleeveless, deep neckline outfits for work.

Appearances play an important role in deciding an individual's personality. An individual who is formally dressed is considered a mature professional who adheres to the organization's dress code and values rules and regulations. She is often taken as a serious individual who would deliver her level best and successfully accomplish tasks assigned to them. One who comes to the office dressed in casuals is often not treated as a serious and sincere employee. Corporate dressing helps you get noticed and stand apart from the rest. Dressing well will not only increase your self-confidence but will also impress and attract other people. Proper grooming and a professional appearance are important **to gain respect in the workplace**. The way you look and carry yourself creates an impression on the people you work alongside.

***"“Looking at you is a pleasant experience, looking like you belong like you know what you're doing, nothing about your appearance is disturbing or distracting. Looking like yourself, the way you want to be seen and feel"***

***- Judith Rasband*"**

# IX

# ACCESSORIZE: THE RIGHT WAY

***"“If there was a choice on spending a lot of money on accessories or dress, I always chose accessories. I think jewellery can change an outfit more than anything else”***
***– Iris Apfel"***

Appearances play an important role in deciding an individual's personality. Whether this is real or imaginary the most important fact is that your appearance influences the opinions of everyone around you. Overall appearance includes your Clothing, Grooming, Hygiene, Makeup, Accessories, Body language and Etiquette.

In previous chapters you learnt about Grooming, Hygiene, Makeup, and Clothing. In this chapter we shall discuss about Accessories and its importance and about accessories suitable for work.

Accessories are like icing on the cake. Any item that completes an outfit and adds polish to the look is considered as Accessory. ***Accessories are of different types like Classic, workday, glamourous, edgy, and casual accessories.*** In this chapter you learn about the essential accessories you wear for work.

Essential accessories used daily include shoes, handbags, neck ties, belts, watches, jewellery, stockings, and other accessories like glasses, hats, gloves, scarves, shawls, pocket squares, hair ornaments, flowers, handkerchiefs should not be overlooked.

## *Importance and Benefits of wearing accessories*

- Accessories should be selected with their purpose and power in mind. Take a moment to think about what each item contributes to the image you want to project.
- An attractive accessory can be just the item that pulls together the look of a new outfit, coordinating with different clothing pieces and creating a finished appearance.
- An eye-catching accessory can lead an observer's eye to a point of emphasis, or a well-placed accessory can divert the observer's gaze away from the areas where you don't want the attention and direct it to the area where you want attention. ***For example***- an interesting neckpiece or Earrings can direct attention towards your face
- Accessories can add interest and variety to an outfit along with sparkle to your style.
- Accessories can upgrade lesser quality clothing, or downgrade even the finest of clothes and your entire

appearance.

- Changing accessories is an excellent way to change the look or message of basic garments, use them to dress yourself UP or Down according to the occasion. You not only look different but also feel different.
- Coordinate or combine clothing and accessories for more effective visual communication, greater versatility, interest, and individuality.
- When selecting accessories, learn to mix and match with clothes you already own, so that you can manage with a few accessories.
- The Colour of accessories and the clothing colour should be in harmony. When you repeat a clothing colour in accessories, that colour becomes more noticeable in the clothes. Make sure it's that colour you want to make more important or dominant.
- If all accessories are of the same colour, it creates monotony. If you use the same colour, then create variety by choosing accessories of different shades or textures.

## *LIST OF ACCESSORIES*

***Here is the list of all the accessories:-***

| LIST OF ACCESSORIES | |
|---|---|
| - Necklaces/chains | - Shoes / sandals |
| - Stoles/ Scarves | - Bags & wallets |
| - Belts | - Briefcase |
| - Watches | - Eyeglasses/ Sunglasses |
| - Bracelet/ Bangles | - Hair Accessories- hair clip, hair band |
| - Earrings | - Hats/ head wear |
| - Brooch | - Cufflinks |
| - Pocket squares | - Gloves |
| - Tie | - Umbrella |
| - Tie pin | - Pen |

Accessories

***Here you learn about a few essential accessories you could wear for work.***

Accessories

## *Essential Accessories - What to wear and What to avoid for work*

### *1. SHOES*

- Shoes should be of good quality leather.
- The shoe colour should be darker than your trouser.
- Shoes should be pumps or slingbacks, do not wear shoes with open toes, open heels, or ankle straps.
- Heels should be 1-2 inches; higher heels should be saved for after hours.
- Avoid wearing shoes with bling for formal occasions.
- Do not wear colourful sandals
- Avoid heels and sandals with bling
- Avoid flip flops and athletic shoes.

## 2. SOCKS

- Choose a colour that coordinates with your trousers (usually black, dark grey, dark brown, or dark blue).
- Make sure they are long enough not to expose your leg's skin when you sit.
- As a thumb rule, do not wear white socks.
- Wear clean socks to avoid bad odour.
- Avoid wearing white socks with black or brown Shoes.
- Avoid wearing printed socks.

## 3. BELTS

- Wear only formal belts with a sleek buckle.
- As a thumb rule, match your belt to your shoes.
- Black or Brown belts are preferred for work
- Avoid belts with chunky buckles.

## 4. JEWELLERY

- Jewellery, when tastefully worn, is always an asset to your outfit.
- For work, wear only one pair of earrings and should be discreet. Ear studs and earloops should not be longer than ½".
- Do not wear big hoops or dangling earrings for work

- You can wear a simple thin necklace. Do not wear ornamental/ chunky jewellery for formal occasions.
- Do not wear big Nose rings and anklets to work.
- Do not wear accessories that are not part of the Dress code.
- You can wear a simple watch to work.
- Wear Only one ring on each hand or a maximum of three rings on both hands and wear simple rings.
- You may wear either a bracelet or a bangle. Avoid wearing both
- Avoid chunky bracelets and wearing too many bangles.

## *5. BAGS*

- Your handbag must go with your outfit and complement your overall look.
- Use Black or Brown coloured Bags/Briefcase.

## *6. WATCHES*

- Preferably wear metal or leather strapped watches.
- If you wear a metal strapped watch, make sure that it fits the wrist well.
- Avoid colourful watches and Sports watches.

## *7. SPECTACLES*

- The spectacles must be simple in design.
- The frame should fit the face of the wearer and should be neither oversized nor undersized.
- Bright colours are not preferred for work.

## *Accessories Tips for Work*

- Jewellery should be kept minimal and conservative
- Remove all facial piercing except earrings
- Body piercings (eyebrow piercings or lip piercings) and tattoos of any kind should be strictly avoided in organizations where work culture is conservative. ("Corporate Dressing for Women Tips to Dress Correctly at ...")
- ***The 5 Piece Rule***: Wear only 5 accessories earrings count as 2; watch counts as 3, allowing 2 additional accessories, maybe neckpiece, or belt or bracelet or watch

Accessories always add interest, variety, and individuality to an outfit. Keeping in mind the goal, and the image you want to project, choose the accessories. Take a moment to think about what each item contributes to the image you want to project and always the accessory should be in harmony with your outfit.

***"“It is the unseen, unforgettable, ultimate accessory of fashion that heralds your arrival and prolongs your departure”***
***– Coco Chanel"***

# X

# PERSONAL GROOMING MYTHS AND ROUTINES

> ***"“When You are living the Best version of Yourself You inspire others to live the best versions of themselves” – Dr. Steve Maraboli"***

In previous chapters, you learnt about the importance of personal grooming and how it helps in your professional and social lives. You have understood the importance of first impression, how your image matters, how clothing and grooming impacts your Appearance and people's perception of you.

You have learnt about the 3 pillars of personal grooming i.e., Grooming and hygiene, Clothing and Accessories and

Skincare and Makeup.

In this book, everything about the first pillar Grooming and hygiene is described elaborately. As the first pillar is the base for a well-groomed personality, if you set this right all other pillars work amazingly well. Here only the important points of the second and third pillars are explained in this book.

## *Myths Associated with Personal Grooming*

You might have come across many myths associated with grooming. Here are a few myths about grooming: -

### *Myth-1. Q -Tips are a safe way to clean out earwax.*

It is a myth. The fact is it is not safe to use Q-tips to clean ears as it can push earwax further into your ear canal. It can also cause damage to the ear like rupturing the eardrum. Ear wax prevents the ear from getting dry and protects it from harmful substances like dirt and bacteria. It's not necessary to clean out your ears, as earwax naturally moves to the outer ear and falls out on its own when you move your jaws while chewing.

### *Myth-2. Squeezing the pimple is the best way to get rid of it.*

Popping the pimple seems like a satisfying quick fix, the fact is it leads to blemishes and scarring. Squeezing of pimples spreads debris, dirt, and bacteria in it to other pores and can cause your skin to look swollen and inflamed. The best way to get rid of pimples is not to touch them and allow them to heal themselves. They go away on their own within a week.

### *Myth-3. Moisturizing Oily Skin is not needed*

The fact is like all other types of skin even oily skin needs moisturizer. Use a light moisturizer for oily skin which curb sebum production within sebaceous glands and maintains hydration of the skin.

### *Myth-4. Brushing your Hair 100 strokes a day makes your hair healthy*

**The fact is b**rushing your Hair 100 strokes every day make it prone to breakage and damage hair follicles instead of improving hair condition. Mild brushing of hair helps in preventing tangles and distributes the hair oil evenly across your scalp. Instead, brush your hair once or twice a day and maintain good hair hygiene.

### *Myth-5. Your hair should be washed daily.*

Fact is it depends on a number of factors like hair type, activity level, pollution, weather etc., You can wash daily if you sweat a lot, or if exposed to pollution, if working in a construction site or if your is too oily. If you wash daily, it can remove natural oil from hair strands and leave them dry and brittle

### *Myth-6. Shaving Makes Hair Grow Thicker and Darker.*

The fact is shaving cuts the tip of the hair bluntly, it does not change the thickness or colour of the hair, but when it grows back it looks thicker and darker

### *Myth-7. Only Dirty Hair gets Lice.*

The fact is you will get lice if you have head-to-head contact with the person having lice, even though your hair is clean.

### *Myth-8. Bad breath is caused because of poor oral hygiene only.*

The fact is you can experience bad breath even if you are brushing twice a day, flossing daily, and gargling with mouthwash daily. Bad breath is caused due to dry mouth, gum disease, sinus conditions, throat infections and stomach problems.

### *Myth-9. Women cannot wear a tie*

A tie and official trousers are known to be part of men's grooming habits is a myth. The fact is a woman can equally make a professional formal statement by wearing a tie and formal trousers which can give her a chic professional look while being a little trendy.

### *Myth-10. Women should not wear men styled formal shoes/ boots or sneakers*

It is assumed that women cannot wear a men specific shoe design is a myth. The fact is if you can mix and match a masculine design sneaker, shoes, boots etc. with your ensemble, you should wear it. It shows your creativity and risk-taking ability with confidence. Women should not be restricted to delicate feminine designs or colours or cuts in footwear.

## *Workable Personal Grooming Planner*

Remember, to remain successful in the workplace, in addition to talent, hard work, dedication, and workplace ethics, you need to take those extra 10 minutes every morning for personal grooming and smart dressing as the success of your career depends on it along with your competency.

Before ending the chapter, I would like to share with you the workable Personal grooming rituals, which you can implement effortlessly by spending a few minutes a day, an hour a week and a few hours a month.

An easy step by step plan for personal grooming is provided below. By following these steps consistently over a period of time you could achieve your goal of becoming a well-groomed person.

***Here is the planner for a complete Personal Grooming routine: -***

- Daily Routine
- Weekly Routine
- Monthly Routine
- Quarterly Routine

## *Daily Grooming Routine*

**Daily Morning routine**

- As soon as you wake up Drink a glass of Lukewarm water
- Practice Oral hygiene
- Practice any type of exercises, Yoga or simple stretches
- Take a shower with warm or cold water
- Follow hygiene tips for Nose, ears & eyes without fail while taking bath
- Cleanse your face with face wash or Cleansing gel
- After bath apply Toner followed by moisturizer to face and body lotion to whole body
- Apply Sunscreen for protecting your skin and lip balm to lips
- Apply makeup as mentioned in makeup chapter
- Follow Hair care practices and wear hairstyle suitable for you
- Wear clean ironed clothes and complementing accessories before heading to work

**Daily Afternoon Routine**

- If needed do, make up touch-ups like applying compact powder or loose powder to look fresh
- Apply lip balm or lipstick if needed
- Comb our hair if it is out of place

**Daily Evening Routine**

- It is advised to take a shower in the evening after a long day of work
- Follow CTM steps – cleansing, toning and moisturizing after you wash your face.
- Apply Anti aging cream or cream for acne treatment or serum based on your skin issues.
- Apply body lotion to hands and legs.

Daily Grooming Routine

## *Weekly Grooming Routine*

**Weekly Routine**

- Exfoliation or Scrubbing – To remove dead cells from whole body use body scrub products after body wash
- For face after cleansing, exfoliate, then tone and moisturize.
- You can also apply face masks suitable for your skin type
- Take head bath by applying oil previous night or 2 hr before taking the shower
- Apply conditioner after cleaning your hair with shampoo
- If needed, you can use hair mask
- You can remove unwanted hair weekly once
- You can also go for whole body oil massage and take bath weekly once
- Nail polish application and trimming nails
- Plan outfits and accessories for the whole week, wash and iron them. Arrange them as coordinated sets

Weekly Grooming Routine

## *Monthly Grooming Routine*

**Monthly Routine**

- Hair removal of legs, hands and underarm by shaving or hair removal cream once a week
- Unwanted hair removal of upper lip, chin hair, and Eyebrows shaping by threading or by using razor
- Face hair removal by waxing or threading
- Monthly once you can do facials suitable for your skin type
- Manicure
- Pedicure
- Wardrobe De cluttering for efficient use of your clothes

Monthly Grooming Routine

## *Quarterly Routine*

**Quarterly Routine**

- Hair cut once in every 6-8 weeks
- Trim your hairs to remove split ends
- Do wardrobe audit - check your clothes for any repair , take out old faded clothes, make a list of items you need to buy and donate wardrobe orphans

Quarterly Grooming Routine

## *Always Check...*

**Once you are ready to leave the house for work always check your appearance in the mirror, back and front and ask yourself...**

- Are you clean and tidy?
- Is your look appropriate for the day ahead?
- Do you look neat?
- Are your teeth free from stains (like food or lipstick stains)?
- Check for hairs and dandruff on your collar and shoulders and brush them off
- Is your hair neat and styled appropriately?
- Are your clothes fitting you properly?

- Are your accessories and outfit are well coordinated?
- Is it appropriate to have bare legs or should you be wearing hosiery?
- Ask yourself, Am I looking well-groomed and polished? ***Be your own judge.***

## *Remember to carry these to work: -*

- Mouth fresheners
- Hand Sanitizer
- Comb and Hair clip or band
- A small mirror
- Roll-on Deodorant
- Women carry compact powder, lip gloss or lipstick and eye pencil or eyeliner.
- Face wipes

Always keep these items in your bag while going to work, you need them to freshen up during the long day of work. Along with these items always carry your beautiful smile, it gives an attractive well-groomed and polished look, and is one of your best assets!

## *One Final thought...*

Appearance/Personal Grooming is ***not everything***, but it is something that should be taken into serious consideration. It is like a cherry on the cake, your talents, competency, knowledge, skills and how you work are equally important.

Appearances influence whether you get the job, the promotion, and other opportunities that may come up in your work and personal life. The reality is, we all judge books by their covers, it is human nature.

You are unique and you are a combination of your skills and experience and how you present yourself to the world. The power of dressing and grooming is that you get to choose to a certain extent how you are viewed, how you are perceived and thought about by others. It gives you a way to communicate in a positive way before you open your mouth. You can use this knowledge to make your cover one that expresses what you want people to know about you.

However, it is good to remember that it is just not about wearing expensive brands, it is about wearing clothes that suit you and your body shape and are in top-notch condition. Ill-fitting wrinkled, torn, faded clothes do not give a good impression regardless of you smelling nice or having a good haircut or shave

I hope the overall impact of personal grooming is clearly understood that when you are well-groomed, you build an image that is liked, admired, and respected by society. A well-groomed person with an amicable personality sets a positive impression. Good grooming gives you confidence and if you know you're looking good you'll be feeling good too. Personal grooming has a great impact not only on your professional lives but also on your personal and social lives as well.

*Now that you have all the tools to look well-groomed and polished, go out and use them to achieve whatever you want in life.*

**" "LOOKING GOOD ISN'T SELF- IMPORTANCE;**
**IT'S SELF -RESPECT"**
**---CHARLES HIX "**

# Did You Enjoy Reading The Art Of Personal Grooming?

Thank You so much for reading ***"The Art of Personal Grooming"***. I am honoured that you have spent some of your time reading the book.

If you enjoyed reading "The Art of Personal Grooming", Would you please leave a short review for the book at Notion Press/Amazon/ Flipcart? A sentence or two about something you liked would mean the world to me. Most importantly your comments will encourage others to give the book a try.

I plan to write about the second and third pillars of grooming elaborately in our upcoming books in the ***"Smart Woman"*** Series. If you'd like to be notified when these books are released, be sure to follow me in any of the social media platforms mentioned the about the author page.

If you have questions or would like to share a grooming tip that has made a difference in your life, please feel free to reach out to me at ***rhythmicimagebramara@gmail.com***. I would love to hear about it!

# Sources And Citiations

**Dear Reader**

I have tried to keep this book error-free. But if errors have crept in do let me know. The images and content used in this book are sourced from various internet sources. I have listed most of the sources below.

Thank you for buying this book

All trademarks and brands referred to in this book are for illustrative purposes only, are the property of their respective owners and are not affiliated with this publication in any way. Any trademarks are being used without permission, and the publication of the trademark is not authorized by, associated with or sponsored by the trademark owner.

Content in this book is from my learnings from Image Consulting Business Institute (ICBI), Books of Judith Rasband, Trainings I conducted at Ample courses, Alison Diploma in makeup artistry course, experience gained while teaching my students and from various books /blogs/ youtube videos, I have read/researched/watched related to the topic.

**Various blogs and internet sources referred -**

www. wikipedia.com
www. alison.com
www. scribd.com
www. slideshare.net
www. elle.com
www. managementstudyguide.com
www. psychology.fandom.com
www. work.chron.com
www. whatsmyquote.com

www.quote.com
www.undefeatedmotivation.com
www.psychologicalscience.org
www.coursehero.com
www. tinytouchups.com
www.onemedical.com

**Image Sources** - royalty-free images from these websites are used in the book

www.pexels.com
www.unsplash.com
www.pixabay.com
www.megastocks.com
www.freepik.com
www.dreamstime.com
www.istockphoto.com
www.google.com

I have tried to capture most of the sources I referred to for writing this book. In case I missed mentioning any source, please let me know. My gratitude to all the knowledge sources and to all my mentors mentioned above.

www.ingramcontent.com/pod-product-compliance
Ingram Content Group UK Ltd.
Pitfield, Milton Keynes, MK11 3LW, UK
UKHW021931200726
13853UKWH00010B/130

9 798886 291322